AMERICAN FOOTBALL

Peter Arnold

Kingfisher Books

Introduction

Until recently American football was unique to
the United States. Now there is television
coverage of the game in countries across the
world.

There are lots of 'jargon' words. These are
shown in bold type where they first appear in
the book. You can check their meanings in the
glossary.

Kingfisher Books, Grisewood & Dempsey Ltd,
Elsley House, 24–30 Great Titchfield Street,
London W1P 7AD

First published in hard cover in 1987 by Kingfisher Books

Reprinted 1987, 1988

© Grisewood & Dempsey Limited 1987

BRITISH LIBRARY CATALOGUING IN PUBLICATION DATA
Arnold, Peter,
    American football.—(Kingfisher factbooks)
    1. Football—Juvenile literature
    I. Title
    796.332   GV950.7

    ISBN 0-86272-291-8

Printed in Portugal by Printer Portuguesa
Phototypeset by Southern Positives and Negatives (SPAN), Lingfield, Surrey

Contents

1: Aim of the game

American football is a game for two teams, each with 11 players on the field. While the aim of the game is to control the ball and score points, something which takes speed and superb teamwork, what oftens counts is the size and strength of the players. More than anything, professional football is a game of violent physical contact.

The ultimate objective is to score more points than the other team. To do this, one side must get a player to the opposing end of the field (or **end zone**) with the ball. If he catches or runs it there he scores a goal – a **touchdown** – worth six points. An extra point can also be scored if the team then kicks the ball between the goal posts, and above the crossbar. This last point is known as a 'touchdown conversion'. The whole scoring system of American football is terrifically complicated. The basic methods for scoring points are shown on page 8.

▶ *The New York Giants in combat with the St Louis Cardinals.*
   American football is a colourful game to watch. It is also one of the most confusing games, until you know some of the rules!

The team which controls the ball at any one time is called the **offence**. As it goes on attack, it is met by the team on **defence**, whose objective is to stop the offence moving the ball down the field and scoring a touchdown.

The offensive team tries to get the ball up the field in a series of moves, called 'plays'. There are two main plays an offence can make. One is called a 'rushing play', in which a player will run with the ball as far as he can until he scores or is tackled to the ground. The other is a 'passing play'. Here a player runs down the field while a teammate, usually the quarterback, throws the ball to him. Having caught it, he then keeps running until he scores or is tackled.

When a player is **tackled** and brought to the ground, that play is finished. The offensive team can try to protect the player carrying the ball by **blocking** any tacklers (see page 46–47).

The team on defence has several ways of stopping the opposing team and so taking possession of the ball itself. A player can **intercept** a passing play with a

Offensive positions

Teams face each other on the field in various ways.

A typical offensive play might have seven players on the front line, as shown here. The numbers on the helmets show you what the players are called.

Defensive positions

A defensive team varies its player positions to meet the challenge from the other side.

This group is a typical defence to the team shown above.

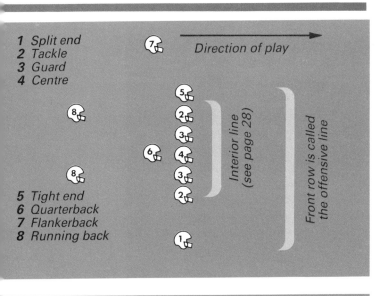

1 Split end
2 Tackle
3 Guard
4 Centre

5 Tight end
6 Quarterback
7 Flankerback
8 Running back

Direction of play

Interior line (see page 28)

Front row is called the offensive line

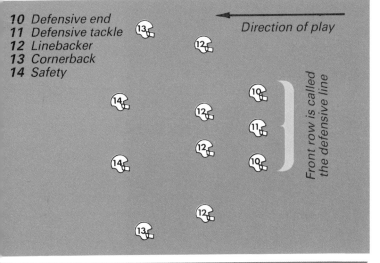

10 Defensive end
11 Defensive tackle
12 Linebacker
13 Cornerback
14 Safety

Direction of play

Front row is called the defensive line

clean catch. He can pick up a ball dropped by a player on the offensive team. Or finally, if the defence can prevent the offence from moving the ball 10 yards up the field within four plays, known as **downs**, it takes over possession of the ball. At this point the two teams switch roles, and the defence becomes the offence.

Professional teams have a set of offence players and a set of defence players, as well as a kicking squad.

Scoring

Score	Points	How achieved
Touchdown	6	*By a runner with the ball crossing the opponents' goal line, or by a player getting possession of a loose ball within the opponents' end zone.*
Extra point	1	*By kicking the ball over the crossbar and between the uprights from a 'line of scrimmage'. This must be done two yards from the opponents' goal line, and only after scoring a touchdown.*
Field goal	3	*By place-kicking the ball over the crossbar and between the uprights, from any position on the field at any time.*
Safety	2	*By tackling an opponent who is carrying the ball behind his own goal line.*

2: The field

The field on which American football is played is commonly called the 'gridiron', because the patterns on it make it look rather like a cooking grill.

The actual field of play is 100 yards long and 160 feet (or 53 yards 1 foot) wide. Lines divide the length of the field into 5-yard strips and, on a National Football League professional pitch, these are numbered every 10 yards from the nearest end zone. The end zone is an area 10 yards deep, between the **end line** and the **goal line**.

There are 1-yard markers along

▼ The American football pitch (5) compared in size to a tennis court (1), a basketball court (2), a rugby pitch (3) and a soccer pitch (4).

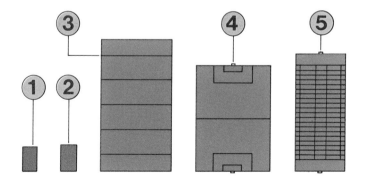

each side of the pitch and in two lines near the centre. These centre lines are called 'inbound lines', or **hash marks**. They are used by officials at the start of a new down, who place or **spot** the ball just inside the nearest hash mark to where the previous play stopped.

The goal post uprights are level with the end line. The uprights are 18 feet 6 inches apart, the same width as the hash marks. The crossbar is 10 feet high.

Last, but not least, there are the goal lines. These are just 8 inches wide and divide the two end zones from the rest of the field. Imagine a sheet of glass standing across a goal line. As soon as the player carrying the ball breaks this imaginary glass sheet, a touchdown is scored. The ball does not have to be actually touched down on the ground.

All the lines along the sides of the pitch are out of bounds to players.

There are two main forms of American football, professional, 'pro' football as described in this book, and college football, played in all the colleges of the United States. There are slight differences in the rules.

The field

The 'gridiron', or American football field. It is always 360 feet long and 160 feet wide, surrounded by a 6 foot wide white border.

▼ *The goal posts are supported by a central stem which is 6 feet behind the end line. The uprights and the crossbar jut forward, however, so that they hang directly above the end line.*

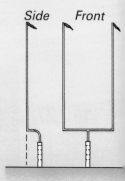

Side   Front

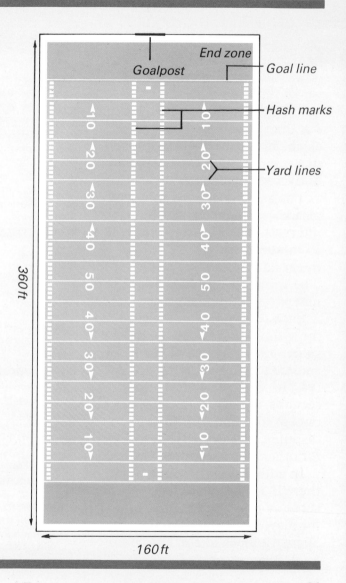

Goalpost

End zone

Goal line

Hash marks

Yard lines

360 ft

160 ft

3: Time factor

A game lasts 60 minutes, but the time is governed by a game clock. This is frequently stopped – so a complete game may not end until three hours after kick-off.

The game is divided into four periods or 'quarters', separated by intervals. The half-time interval is 15 minutes, and the other two intervals are both two minutes. The teams change ends after the first and the third intervals.

Each team can stop the clock three times in each half of the game. These are called **time-outs** and are usually taken for tactical reasons. A time-out lasts for 90 seconds. Officials can call time-outs at any time – for injury, disputes, and so on. See caption for other clock-stopping reasons.

In addition to the game clock, there is a 30-second clock. This is set in motion when the ball is ready for play. An offence team must not allow the clock to run out before beginning the next play.

▶ Cheerleaders keep up the enthusiasm of fans and teams alike. They are almost as much a part of American football as the players themselves!

• The game clock is also stopped after a score, an incomplete pass, an out-of-bounds, a yellow penalty flag, and for the **two-minute warning** – an indication to both teams that only two minutes remain of a half or a game.

4: How the game began

American football started at Harvard University in the 1870s. At that time, American colleges played a game similar to English soccer. In 1874, Harvard played against McGill University of Montreal. The Canadians played a game which was more like English rugby – instead of kicking the ball, they ran with it. Harvard liked this version of the game and persuaded Yale University to play it too. Princeton and Columbia soon followed suit, and in 1876 the Intercollegiate Football Association was formed.

A Yale student and footballer, Walter C. Camp, devised many of the rules of the game, and became known as the 'Father of American football'. He reduced the number of players to 11 and turned the rugby scrummage into a **scrimmage** in 1880.

Two years later he invented the system of downs, and so made the gridiron field necessary. Camp also

▶ Early players had little of the special protection worn by the teams of today.

Many players even refused to wear helmets until they were made compulsory, after World War II.

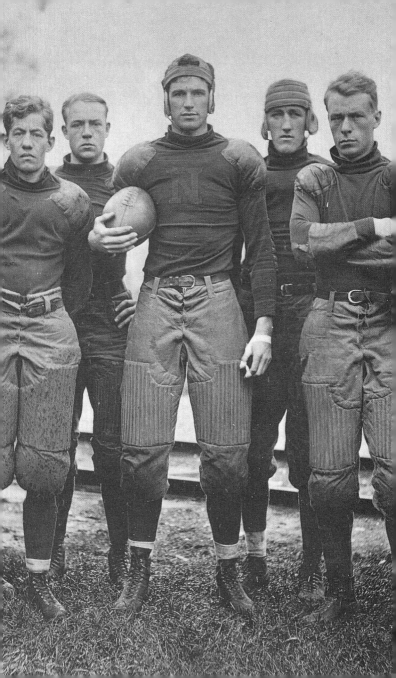

American Football Conference

Eastern Division	Central Division	Western Divison
Buffalo Bills	Cincinnati Bengals	Denver Broncos
Indianapolis Colts	Cleveland Browns	Kansas City Chiefs
Miami Dolphins	Houston Oilers	Los Angeles Raiders
New England Patriots	Pittsburgh Steelers	San Diego Chargers
New York Jets		Seattle Seahawks

devised a scoring system, not unlike today's. The Princeton team then invented blocking and the new game became recognizably American football.

Professional football started when local town football teams began paying the best college graduates to play for them. The National Football League (NFL) was formed in 1921.

In 1960, the formation of the American Football League set up a

▲ The 28 teams of the NFL. In the regular season, a team plays home and away games against all the other teams in its division. It also plays other teams from its own conference, and two to four games against rival conference teams.

National Football Conference

Eastern Division	Central Division	Western Division
Dallas Cowboys	Chicago Bears	Atlanta Falcons
New York Giants	Detroit Lions	Los Angeles Rams
Philadelphia Eagles	Green Bay Packers	New Orleans Saints
St Louis Cardinals	Minnestoa Vikings	San Francisco 49ers
Washington Redskins	Tampa Bay Buccaneers	

strong challenge to the NFL. The two leagues competed heavily to buy the best players, until they merged in 1970. The new NFL then divided the teams into the American Football Conference and the National Football Conference. Each conference has three divisions who play against each other for the conference championships. The two winning conference teams then play for the world championship. This final game is the 'Super Bowl'.

▼ The symbol of the National Football League, the principal league in pro football.

◄ Artificial turf is used on many football fields. It is an all-weather plastic playing surface, which doesn't turn to thick mud if the weather turns rainy. Neither does it need the special care that grass fields require. A skidding fall on artificial turf can cause nasty burns though.

Here, the New York Giants play the St Louis Cardinals.

19

5: Equipment

In the early days of American football, players dressed like the soccer players of the day, in shirts, shorts and boots. However, as tackling and blocking became more and more important, the game grew steadily more violent. A tactic called the 'flying wedge', in which the whole team formed a V-shape around the ball and charged upfield, caused havoc. After 18 players had died, with hundreds injured, President Roosevelt in 1906 threatened to have the game stopped. Forms of 'interlocking interference formations' were banned. Princeton adopted leather helmets. Nowadays the NFL rules insist that helmets and various protective pads are worn.

It now takes a player as long to climb into his protective clothing as it might an actor to make up for a movie. Not all players wear the same protection however, it varies with playing position and personal preference.

▶ Dressing up is an important part of the game, as proper protection is essential.

A team can use over 250 miles of protective tape each season – a player may have 10 yards of tape wrapped around his ankles. Taping up needs skill and is done by the trainers.

Padding up is the next job. Various arrangements of pads and protectors are used.

Dressing to win

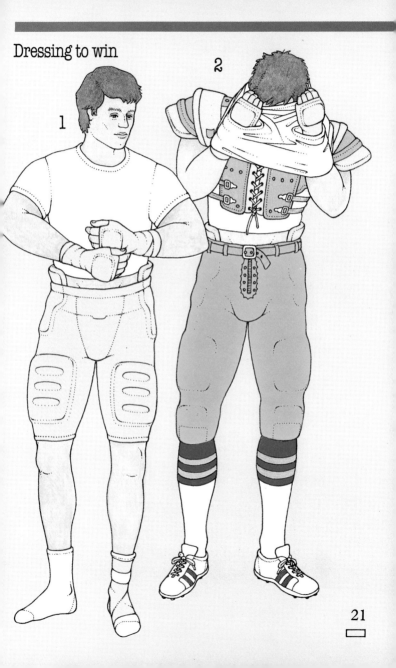

1

2

3

4

22

◄ Shoulder pads create the top-heavy look of American footballers. They are made of plastic, rubber and vinyl.

Helmets last about three season's rough and tumble before they are retired, looking battered and worn.

▼ Shoes are among the last items to be put on. The ones shown here are suitable for (from left to right) grass fields, artificial turf and for kicking.

Let's see what a player could wear. His dressing routine might start with a jockstrap and a plastic box to protect his groin. Then he puts on a tee-shirt and a lot of tape to protect joints like wrists, ankles, fingers and knees. Players might tape different parts – some tape their thumbs to their hands to prevent them holding on to opponents illegally.

He might pull elasticated strengtheners over his elbows and knees – knee braces have metal ribs and joints like a corset. Nylon pants contain pockets to take thigh and knee pads. Shin pads might also be worn.

On the upper body a foam collar protects the neck. Shoulder pads

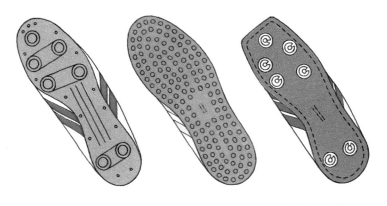

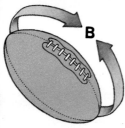

▲ The ball is made of pebble-grained leather. It is 21–21½ inches around the middle (A) and 28–28½ inches around its length (B).

fit over the head, tying at the front. These can weigh 6lb on a lineman, and give the American footballer his distinctive top-heavy shape. He might also wear rib and kidney padding, sometimes extending down his back as part of the shoulder-pad equipment. Some players wear a spine protector.

Down the arms there could be upper arm pads, elbow pads, and forearm pads. An offensive lineman might wear 'gloves' over the back of his hands and fingers.

Over all this, the player will put on his team uniform – shirt, pants, socks and shoes. Footballers now have different shoes for different field surfaces. Each NFL player will have a range of shoes to choose from. Kickers sometimes even play in bare feet.

Mouthguards and noseguards are common. Spectacle wearers can get reinforced plastic glasses and some players paint black streaks under the eyes to reduce glare.

All our player needs now is his helmet, the most glamorous piece of equipment, as it carries the colours and badge of the team.

Colourful helmets

All teams have their own colours and badges. The Houston Oilers include an oil rig as their team symbol – Houston is famous as a Texas oil town.

New York Jets

Pittsburgh Steelers

Los Angeles Raiders

Washington Redskins

Chicago Bears

Los Angeles Rams

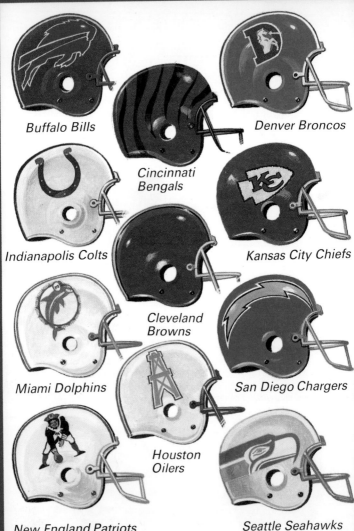

Buffalo Bills

Denver Broncos

Cincinnati
Bengals

Indianapolis Colts

Kansas City Chiefs

Cleveland
Browns

Miami Dolphins

San Diego Chargers

Houston
Oilers

New England Patriots

Seattle Seahawks

Dallas Cowboys

San Francisco
49ers

Minnesota Vikings

New York Giants

Detroit Lions

Tampa Bay Buccaneers

Philadelphia Eagles

Green Bay
Packers

Atlanta Falcons

St Louis Cardinals

New Orleans Saints

6: The start of play

The game begins with a kick-off (see page 33), but imagine that the player who caught the ball has been tackled and play has been stopped. The umpire has placed, or spotted, the ball inside the hash marks. The position of the ball creates an imaginary line across the field, called the **line of scrimmage**. The two teams are positioned on either side of the 'line' in a standard formation like the one shown in the illustration.

The offence must have at least seven men in the offensive line. The centre has his hand on the ball, ready to begin play. On each side of him are guards and outside the guards are tackles. These five are called the 'interior line'. They are the heavies who will protect the player with the ball by blocking tackles from the defence.

Next to the left-hand tackle in the example is the tight end. Far to the right, is the seventh man in the offensive line, the split end. Far to

Offensive team

▲ The teams face each other at the line of scrimmage. There is no actual line – it is simply the point where a play begins. It runs through the ball from sideline to sideline.

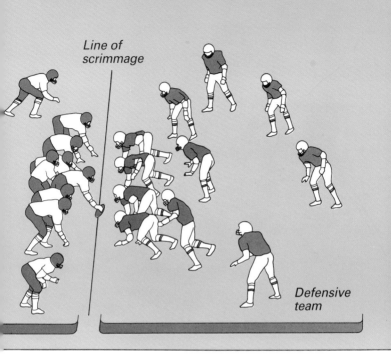

Line of
scrimmage

Defensive
team

the left, but standing further back, is a flankerback. The split end and flankerback are fast runners who will penetrate the defence in expectation of receiving a pass. They are also called 'wide receivers'.

Just behind the centre is the quarterback, who 'calls the play' to the other players by shouting out a series of numbers or code words, which describe to his team what

▲ *The defensive team can move around at will. However, no player can cross the line of scrimmage, or be in the 11-inch wide neutral zone between the two lines of players, until the snap is taken.*

▲ *The snap is shown here.*
1 The centre has his hand on the ball, ready to snap
2 The ball is passed (snapped) to the quarterback waiting behind

the play will be. These codes are all agreed beforehand.

The centre **snaps** the ball between his legs to the waiting quarterback. If the play is a passing play, the interior linemen will form a pocket around the quarterback to give him time to spot a player to whom he can pass the ball accurately.

Alternatively, the play might be a running play. Behind the quarterback are the last two offensive players, the powerful

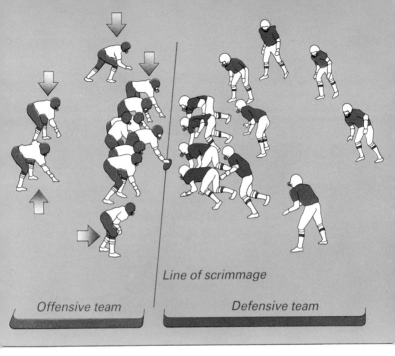

Line of scrimmage

Offensive team

Defensive team

running backs. The quarterback could hand the ball to one of them to try to run through the defence. The interior line will now attempt to block tackles on the running back.

The defensive formation is planned to counter the offensive play. In the front line are the 'defensive linemen', usually two tackles flanked by two ends. They attempt to rush the quarterback or tackle the running back. In the

▲ *Not all offensive players are allowed to catch a forward pass. Those who can do so are arrowed here.*

Any defensive player may intercept a pass and run with the ball.

second row are the three 'linebackers'. Their task is to quickly spot the offensive play and tackle a runner or intercept the ball on a pass, as necessary.

The last line of defence are the **defensive backs** or **secondary** defenders. The two middle players are safeties, the outside ones cornerbacks. Their first task is to defend against a passing play, but they might be needed to tackle running backs, too.

▲ *Small, thin players would not be seen wearing a shirt number like this!*

The defence are allowed to move at will before the snap, and frequently do so to confuse the offence. The offence is more restricted – only one man is allowed to move, and only sideways. You often see the flankerback running across the field to a position on the opposite flank, but he is not allowed to run forwards before the ball is snapped.

Only certain players in the offence are allowed to receive a pass. Players on either side of the offensive line are eligible and so are those at least one yard behind the line at the snap. The rest are not eligible.

32

Players' shirt numbers

All NFL players are numbered according to their positions in their teams. The numbering system is:

1-19 Quarterbacks and kickers

20-49 Running backs and defensive backs

50-59 Centres and linebackers

60-79 Defensive linemen and interior offensive linemen

80-89 Wide receivers and tight ends

90-99 Defensive linemen. (These numbers are in addition to 60-79)

Some rules

• A kick-off is when the kicker place-kicks the ball from his team's 35-yard line. The kicking team must be behind the kicker and cannot touch the ball until it has travelled 10 yards or the receiving team has touched it.
• Only one forward pass is permitted in each down. It can be thrown only by a player who has not crossed the line of scrimmage, and caught only by an eligible receiver. Any member of the defence may intercept.
• If nobody catches a pass, or the ball goes out of bounds, the pass is 'incomplete' and the ball dead. The ball is returned to the line of scrimmage and the offence loses a down.
• Penalties are usually the loss of a down, or the loss of territory – 5, 10 or 15 yards.

7: Strategy and tactics

The head coach is a powerful and famous man in American football. He not only inspires, trains and almost mothers the team, he is also in overall control of the strategy, even during the game. He has assistant coaches, and often leaves the details of a particular aspect of the game to a specialist assistant – a defensive organizer, for instance. But he will be on the

▼ *Running backs often receive passes. In deciding which route to then take with the ball, the first problem is whether to run through or go around the other side. Here are some common routes with their names.*

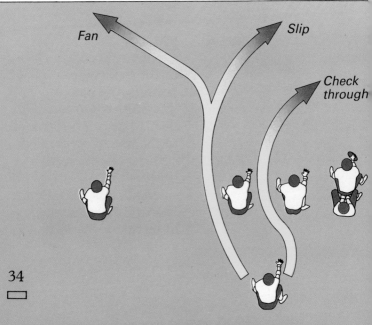

Fan

Slip

Check through

sidelines during a game and
usually gives the quarterback
the **signal** for the next play.

The quarterback receives the
signal and calls the team into a
huddle, a few yards behind the
line of scrimmage. He tells the
players their formation and the
play by means of a code, for
example, 'Red, Left, 20'. He also
decides the count on which the
snap is to be made.

When the offensive line is
formed he calls out his
instructions, for example, 'Red 20,
red 20, set, hut, hut . . .' and if the

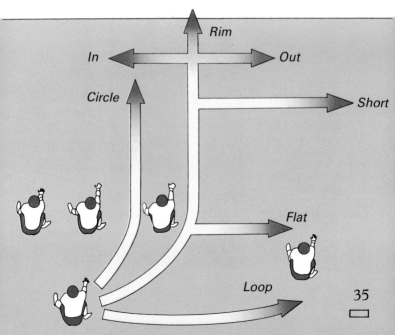

35

Offensive formations

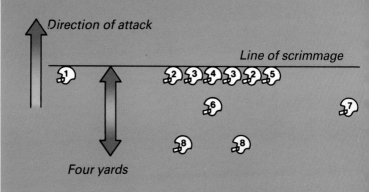

Direction of attack

Line of scrimmage

Four yards

Pro set formation

Key to numbers
on diagrams:
1 Split end
2 Tackle
3 Guard
4 Centre
5 Tight end
6 Quarterback
7 Flankerback
8 Running back
9 Halfback

second 'hut' is the pre-arranged one, the ball is snapped. He might, when he sees the defensive formation, change the play at the line of scrimmage, in which case he might call, 'Red 20, red 20, brown 18, brown 18, set, hut, hut . . .'

The two main tactics for an offence at a down are to rush or pass. The quarterback gets the ball to a running back by placing it in his hands, called a **handoff**, or by a

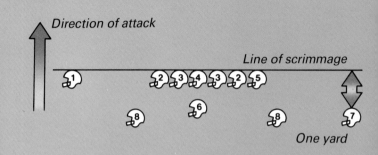

Direction of attack

Line of scrimmage

One yard

Spread set formation

short pass, **pitchout**. The back's
run might be 'up the middle',
'inside' (between the offensive
tackles) or 'outside' (around the
offensive tackle).

Running backs are also expected
to make runs on a passing play.
Their runs begin from behind the
offensive line.

The offence might vary its
formation during a game, both for
specific plays and to keep the
defence guessing. The standard

▲ *A spread set
formation. The five
eligible receivers
(split end, tight
end, two running
backs and
flankerback) all
have clear paths
into the defence's
territory ready for a
pass play.*

Offensive formations

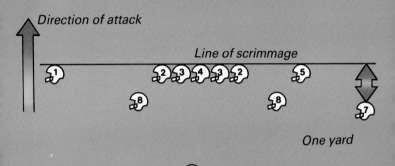

Direction of attack

Line of scrimmage

One yard

Shotgun formation

▲ *You can spot the shotgun formation by the quarterback dropping back to take a long snap. It is a popular formation when the team has to go for a passing play.*

pro **set** formation is one that gives no clues to the defence, as it is equally suitable for passing or rushing.

The 'spread set' formation moves the running backs further apart and closer to the line of scrimmage. This is very suitable for a passing play, as five players are in a good position to receive a pass.

The 'shotgun' formation is an exaggerated spread, which

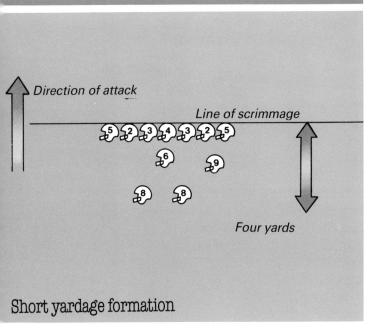

Direction of attack

Line of scrimmage

Four yards

Short yardage formation

regained some popularity in the
late 1970s. The tight end moves
wider of the offensive linemen and
the quarterback comes deep to
some 5 or 7 yards behind the
centre. The snap here is more
difficult, but the quarterback has
maximum passing opportunities.
A good running play, however, is
almost impossible.

A 'short yardage' formation
almost always commits the team to
the rush. There are no split ends or

▲ *The 'short
yardage' formation
has no split ends or
wide receivers.*

wide receivers in the formation. A running back may attempt to jump over the mass of tangled linemen to gain the yard or two required for the down.

The defence, of course, will position themselves to stop the offensive. Against the short yardage offence they might adopt a 7-1-3 formation. A seven-man defensive line, with five tackles and two ends, will attempt to become an immovable wall, while a minimum of defensive backs will guard against a running back coming round on the loop.

Its opposite, the 3-1-7 'penny' defence is deployed against an offence needing to gain plenty of yards. It covers the secondary defensive area and allows many tacklers to converge on a rush.

The 4-2-5, or 'nickel' defence, is similar, providing five defensive backs to guard against a passing play. The 4-1-6, or 'dime' defence brings another linebacker deep into the pass defence zone.

The 4-3-4 is a standard all-purpose formation, with the three linebackers being ready to adapt to any offensive play.

The same number key is used here fo the attacking formations as that shown on previou pages.
 Here is the key for the defending teams shown here and over the page
 10 *Defensive end*
 11 *Defensive tackle*
 12 *Cornerback*
 13 *Lineback*
 14 *Safety*

▶ *The 7-1-3 formation provide a strong defensive line with five tackles to defend short-yardage play. It is possible that a running bac will attempt to div over the line.*
 The 3-1-7 penny defence is adopted when the offence needs a lc of yardage for a first down.

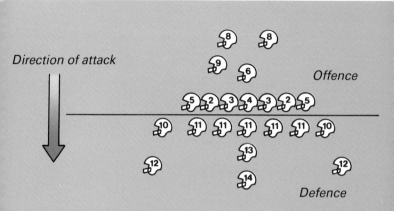

Direction of attack

Offence

Defence

The 7-1-3 formation

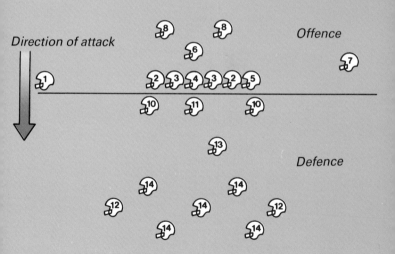

Direction of attack

Offence

Defence

The 3-1-7 'penny' defence

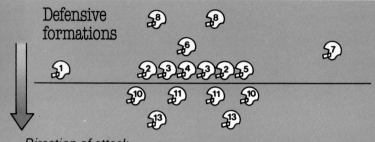

Defensive formations

Direction of attack

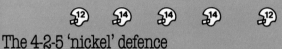

The 4-2-5 'nickel' defence

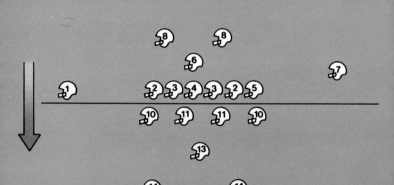

The 4-1-6 'dime' defence

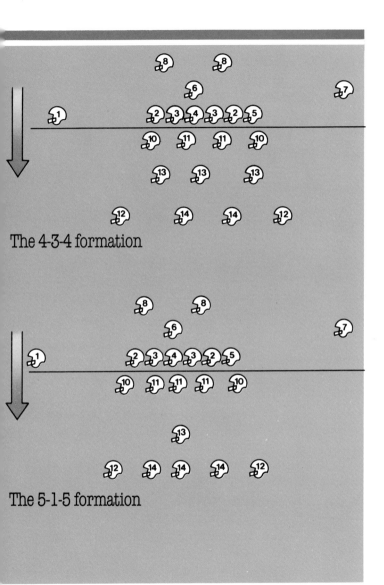

The 4-3-4 formation

The 5-1-5 formation

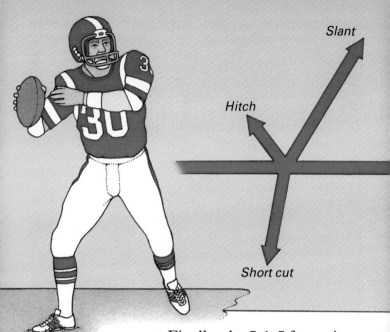

Slant

Hitch

Short cut

Finally, the 5-1-5 formation provides a maximum of defensive linemen to rush the quarterback with plenty of pass defenders. But the single linebacker has plenty to do if a running back gets clear.

The situation of the game often dictates a choice of play, particularly near the end of a match. A team on offence and less than three points behind their opponents will possibly try to get into a good **field-goal** position, taking up as much time as possible,

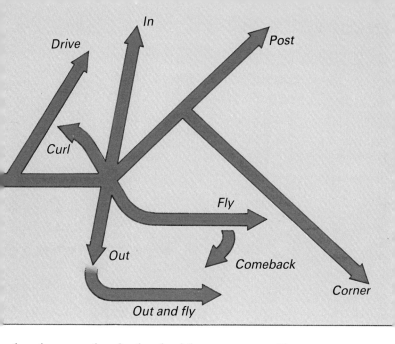

Drive

In

Post

Curl

Fly

Out

Comeback

Corner

Out and fly

hoping to take the lead with a three-point score while denying the opposition much time to reply.

A side needing lots of points will attempt to make ground quickly. They will play the ball near the lines, so that a runner or receiver can step out of bounds to stop the clock. Sometimes the quarterback will throw the ball out of play, which stops the clock and allows new tactics to be discussed. If the offensive team is winning near the end, it will use the allowed 30 seconds on each down.

▲ *The passing tree. Every eligible pass receiver has a pass pattern. When they are all drawn together they look like the branches and twigs of a tree.*

8: Watching the players at work

The quarterback is the focal point of American football. He throws the passes, and a long touchdown pass is an exciting sight as the ball spins through the sky.

The wide receivers are fast – sometimes Olympic sprinters – and they must also be able to catch. The running backs are the strong men who take the ball, and the knocks as the defence bring them down. The offensive linemen are often the biggest players. They protect the quarterback and block potential tacklers.

The defensive players mirror the offence – the tackles and ends are big; the cornerbacks and safeties fast and agile; the linebackers are the strong, mobile all-rounders.

There are also **special teams**, players who only come onto the field at certain points. Of these, the place-kicker can win games with a late field goal. The punter takes the long defensive **punts** or kicks downfield.

▶ Blocking is a legitimate tactic that is illegal in most other forms of football. The blocker protects a colleague with the ball by blocking would-be tacklers.

A blocker may use any part of his body except hands or feet. The top illustration shows a body block, where the blocker has thrown his body across the path of an opponent.

▶ It is illegal to block from behind. Throwing the body across the back of an opponent (right) is known as 'clipping'. It is a dangerous personal foul and is penalized by the loss of 15 yards.

Blocking and clipping

Tackling

A tackler uses his body and arms to bring down a ball carrier, usually trying to hit his man with his shoulder and wrap his arms around his legs. Several tacklers might pile in together to stop a strong runner.

Punting

Punting is used when an offence team is unlikely to make a **first down** (the first 10 yards). The punter takes the ball after the snap, remains cool as the defence charges, and kicks the ball high while his team gets as far upfield as possible.

Running with the ball

The runner must make as much ground as he can, protecting the ball under one arm while fending off tacklers with the other. His blockers help him. He must not fumble the ball when tackled, as the defence may claim it.

Passing and Pass Receiving

The passer throws to a receiver, who must try to help by running into a good unmarked position, often agreed beforehand with the passer. It is an expensive error for a pass to be intercepted as the offensive team loses the ball.

9: The officials

Seven officials control a football game. The referee is the head official and is generally in charge. He stands behind the line of scrimmage and the action around the quarterback is his chief responsibility. He signals any penalties to the spectators.

The umpire stands opposite the referee, behind the defensive line. He watches the offensive and defensive line play. He spots the ball after each down. He is also responsible for checking the players' equipment.

The head linesman stands on the line of scrimmage to the left of the offence and watches out for players crossing the scrimmage line. He is in charge of the **chain crew** who mark the downs (see page 57).

The line judge is at the opposite end of the line of scrimmage to the head linesman. He judges play on his side of the field. He also keeps a

► *The referee tells players and watchers of his decisions using a complex system of hand signals.*

1 *Touchdown, field goal or try*
2 *Safety*
3 **Dead ball** *or* **neutral zone** *established*
4 *Time out*
5 *Ball illegally touched, kicked or batted*
6 *Game delayed*
7 *No time out, or time in with whistle*
8 **Offside** *or crossing the line*
9 *Illegal use of hands, arms, or body*
10 *Pass juggled or caught out of bounds*
11 *Illegal forward pass*
12 *Interference with forward pass or fair catch*

52

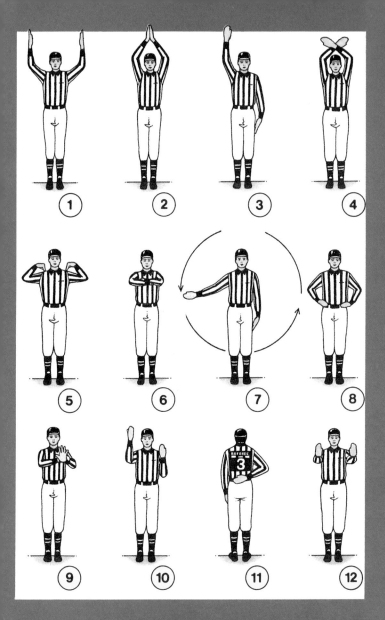

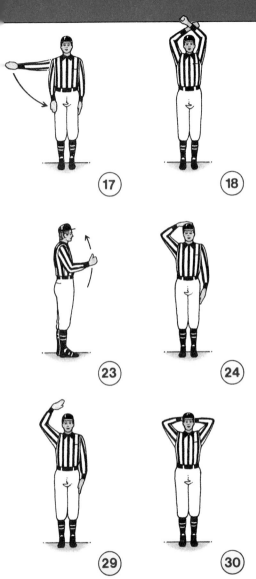

(17) (18)

(23) (24)

(29) (30)

13 Illegal motion at the snap
14 Crawling, pushing or helping runner
15 Unsportsman-like conduct (non-contact fouls)
16 Tripping
17 Illegal crackback
18 Personal foul
19 Illegal contact
20 Intentional grounding of a pass
21 Illegal cut, blocking below waist
22 Touching a forward pass, or a scrimmage kick
23 Player disqualified
24 Ineligible receiver or member of kicking team downfield
25 False start, illegal shift, procedure or formation
26 First down
27 Holding
28 Penalty refused, incomplete pass, play over or missed field goal
29 Invalid **fair catch**
30 Loss of down

game clock as a back-up for the score-board clock.

The back judge stands in the defensive backfield on the same side as the line judge, but some 15 to 17 yards further down, and rules on pass plays on his side of the field.

The side judge is the equivalent of the back judge on the other side. He stands some 15 to 17 yards further down than the head linesman on the defensive side.

The field judge stands deepest, some 22 to 25 yards downfield on the defensive side. He is not directly behind the umpire but is towards the head linesman's side. He watches for the legality of blocks and catches, pass interference and **clipping**. He acts as back-up to the 30-second clock.

Each official carries a yellow piece of cloth with a weight in one corner, called a flag, and he throws it on the field – a **flag down** – when he spots an infringement.

Since 1986, officials have been allowed to use instant video replays in disputes. But video can be used only occasionally and would delay the action if over-used.

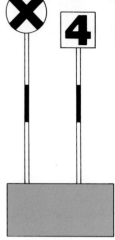

▲ These indicators are used on the sidelines to mark the line of scrimmage and the number of the down.

▶ The chain measuring equipment is used if there is any doubt about a 10-yard gain in a first down. The chain crew appear, and use the equipment to measure the distance from the previous line of scrimmage to the point where play has ended.

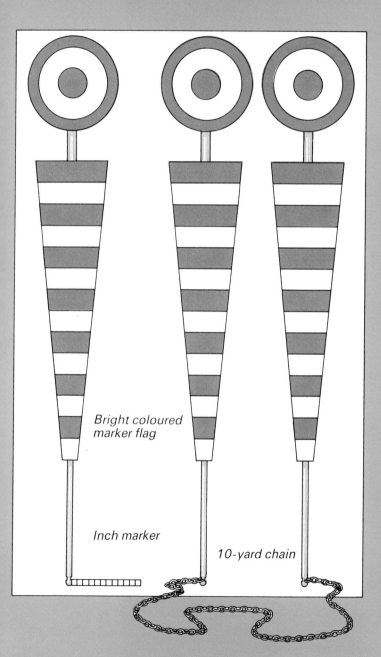

Bright coloured
marker flag

Inch marker

10-yard chain

10: Where they play

Some of the NFL stadia are among the best in the world. Each stadium holds at least 50,000 spectators, many are covered, and electronic score-boards keep fans informed, and even show instant TV replays of big plays. All have ample car parking; you can buy food, and soft drinks, and the whole event is treated as a family outing.

Just under half of the pitches are grass, while the others are artificial turf – Astroturf, Tartan Turf or

▼ The size of stadia varies. The two below are medium sized. On the left is the Chicago Bears' Soldier Field, with room for 65,790. On the right, the Green Bay Packers' Lambeau Field has room for 57,063.

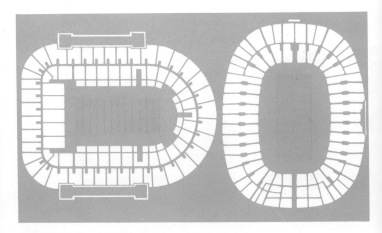

some similar synthetic surface.

One famous stadium is the Louisiana Superdome, home of the New Orleans Saints and a regular Super Bowl venue. It took four years to build and cost $163 million. The Houston Oilers play in their Astrodome, the Seatle Seahawks in their Kingdome. The Lions, Vikings and Colts also have their own domes.

The open-air Orange Bowl in

▲ *Electronic scoreboards give the fans many details of play as well as the score.*

Miami is now fifty years old, and the Dolphins are building a new stadium. Moving to a new stadium always causes problems among fans. When the Oakland Raiders became the Los Angeles Raiders in 1982 and moved to the Memorial Coliseum (where the 1984 Olympics were held) they were challenged in the courts.

The Chicago Bears have the oldest stadium, at Soldier Field. This was the scene of another famous sporting event, the Dempsey-Tunney heavyweight boxing fight in 1927, watched by over 100,000.

American football is not all glamour, however. At the 1986 play-off game with the Giants, the weather was so cold, the teams had frostbite treatment units standing by, just in case!

▶ The officials dress in black and white striped shirts.
   Six of the officials wear white caps. Only the referee wears a black cap.

11: TV and promotion

American football has been a popular spectator sport since it began, over a hundred years ago. The first Rose Bowl game (a college championship) at Pasadena, in 1902, was watched by over 20,000 fans. But it was the 1959 NFL championship game which put the current boom on the road. The Baltimore Colts beat the New York Giants 23–17 in overtime, and millions of American television viewers were glued to their screens.

The television companies wooed the NFL with offers worth millions of dollars. Oil millionaire Lamar Hunt launched the American Football League in competition. It did badly until 1964, when the Columbia Broadcasting System (CBS) outbid the National Broadcasting Corporation (NBC) for the NFL rights. CBS paid $16 million in that season, for a game a week. NBC immediately struck a $36

▶ *The NFL sells all sorts of enthusiast gear, including team sweatshirts and even a team towel, printed in Los Angeles Raiders' colours.*

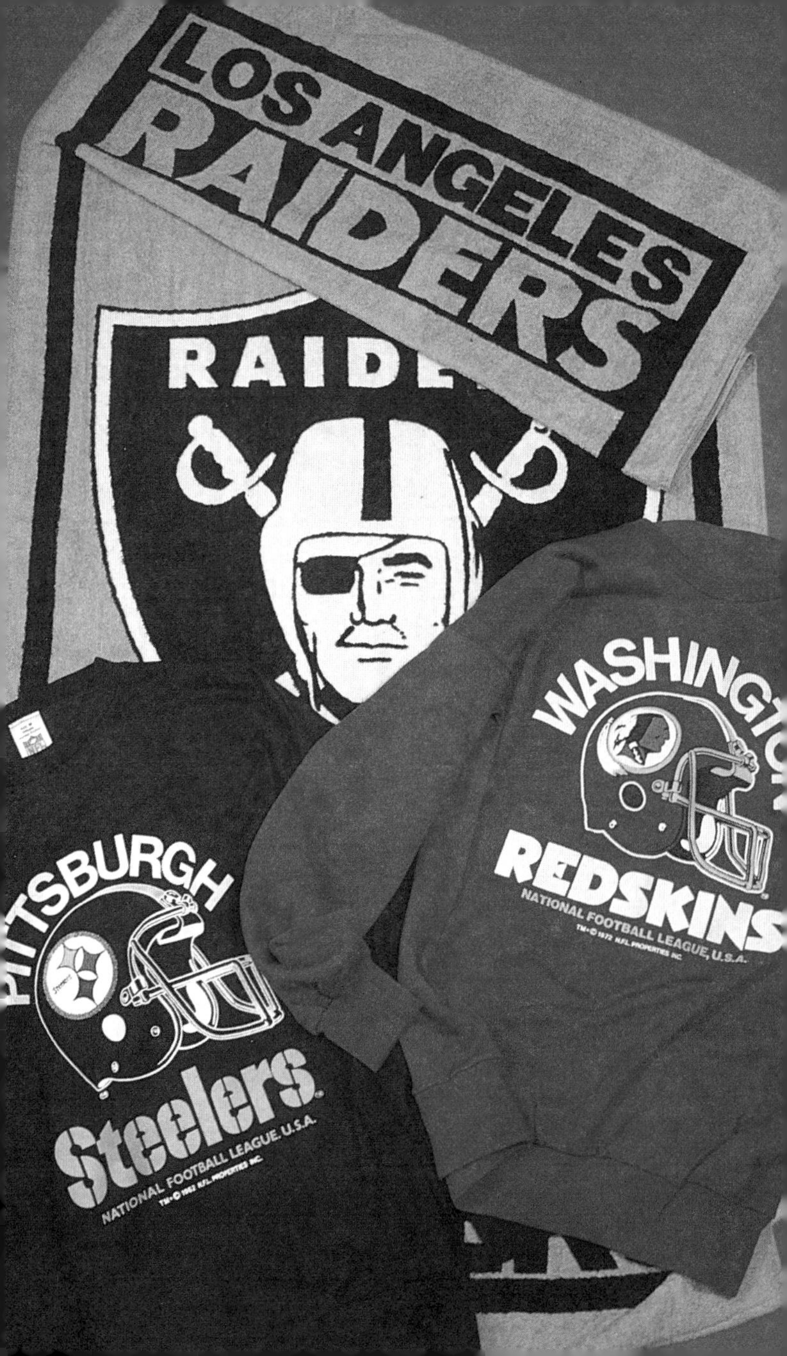

LOS ANGELES
RAIDERS
RAIDE
WASHINGTON
REDSKINS
NATIONAL FOOTBALL LEAGUE, U.S.A.
PITTSBURGH
Steelers
NATIONAL FOOTBALL LEAGUE, U.S.A.

million five-year contract with AFL.

Pete Rozelle, the NFL commissioner, used the TV money to strengthen the league. But many people had misgivings, fearing that TV would take over the game. Indeed, referees today do call time-out to suit advertising schedules. However, when the NFL and the AFL merged, Rozelle persuaded NBC, CBS and ABC (American Broadcasting Corporation) to agree to share coverage. The television audience grew, and by the early 1970s the rights to the Super Bowl alone were costing the TV companies $2.5 million.

Rozelle's strategy was immensely successful. Nowadays, a determined fan can see every minute of every game on television. And the alliance between the game and television seemed complete in 1986, when referees were allowed to use instant TV playbacks to help make decisions on the field.

The use of television has also had an enormous effect on the rest of the world's attitude to the game. A good example of this can be seen in Britain.

▲ *American football has left the shores of the United States. Here, Tampa plays Philadelphia at Wembley, London, in 1984.*

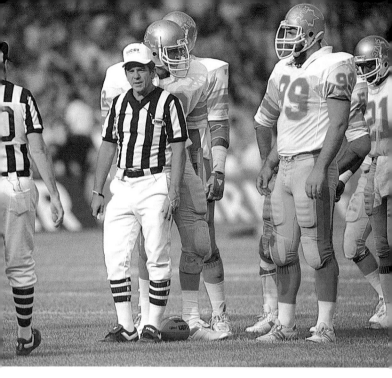

Channel 4 Television began in autumn 1982. Each Sunday they showed an hour's highlights of the previous week's American football games. It was good cheap television. It was also hugely successful. In the first season, British audiences grasped the rules well enough for two million viewers to sit up in the small hours to watch the Super Bowl live. In three years this audience increased to 10 million. When the NFL sent

▲ *The symbol of the 21st Super Bowl series. Each season, the winners of the AFC and NFC meet in the Super Bowl.*

over the Chicago Bears and the Dallas Cowboys to play at Wembley in 1986, a crowd of 82,000 saw the match.

In a little over three years, over 200 British clubs have been set up. There are now three leagues: the Budweiser League, the British American Football League and the Amateur American Football Conference. It is the same story elsewhere; most European and Far Eastern countries have their own teams.

▶ *William 'the Refrigerator' Perry plays for the Chicago Bears. He is currently one of the best known players in American football.*

He is so big, his manager complains, his socks can only be used once – they stretch too much to be used again!

The image that is presented of American football is a forceful one. The game at first looks like organized mayhem, but the officials have absolute control, and there is no viciousness. Everybody is seated. The stadia are clean and airy. The Super Bowl is like a holiday, with reunions and family picnics. Television exposure has not reduced crowds, it has encouraged viewers to add to them, enjoying a day out by going to matches 'live'.

The TV promotion of American Football has been like a throw by Joe Montana (of the San Francisco 49ers) homing into the end zone.

12: Facts and records

Here are a few of the facts and records which have been noted over the years.

Biggest scores
The biggest victory in American football was by the college team, Georgia Tech, in 1916. They defeated Cumberland 222-0. The NFL record was set on 27 November 1966, when the Washington Redskins beat the New York Giants 72-41, the highest points score by one side.

Least successful team
The least successful team currently in the NFL are New Orleans Saints. Since they were founded in 1967 they have never ended a season with more wins than defeats.

Most successful team
The Green Bay Packers are unique in the NFL. They are the only publicly-owned team and the only one in their original town. Formed in 1919, as a works team of the Acme Packing Company, they have won two Super Bowls and nine other champion-ships. However, they are currently not doing well.

Biggest and smallest players
The tallest players in 1986 in the NFL were Dallas Cowboys' Ed 'Too Tall' Jones and Phil Poderac, who each

measured 6 ft 9 in. The shortest was the Cincinnati Bengal's kicker Jim Breech, at 5 ft 6 in. The heaviest was the New Orleans Saints' tackle Angelo Fields, whose 314 lb outweighs 'The Refrigerator', William Perry, by 7 lb. A Cincinnati Bengal player of the past, Dick Sligh, was reckoned to be 7 ft tall, Reggie 'The Elf' Smith, Atlanta Falcons kicker, measured 5 ft 4 in.

▲ *Dick Sligh and Reggie 'The Elf' Smith, tallest and shortest football players.*

Shortest touchdown pass

In 1960, Dallas Cowboys lined up 2 inches from the Washington Redskins' goal line. Quarterback Eddie LeBaron passed to Dick Bielski, who scored a touchdown. Thus the touchdown pass was a 'two-incher', the shortest ever recorded.

Super Bowl wild card

In 1981, Oakland Raiders became the first team to win the Super Bowl from a wild card entry – they were given a place in the play-offs on a 'best-loser' principle. The following year the Raiders moved to Los Angeles and became the Los Angeles Raiders.

Longest losing run

The last two teams elected to the NFL were the Seattle Seahawks and the Tampa Bay Buccaneers in 1976. The Buccaneers must have wondered what they were letting themselves in for. They lost their first 26 matches, still the longest consecutive losing run in the NFL.

Coldest game

The coldest game in the NFL was probably at Cincinnati in 1982, when the Bengals played the San Diego Chargers in the AFC Championship game. The temperature was − 35°C. Ken Anderson, the Cincinnati quarterback, suffered frostbite in one ear. Consolation for him, and those fans who could survive the conditions, was that he led the Bengals to a 27-7 victory.

Most fanatic fan

College football's most astonishing fan is Giles Pellerin, from San Marino, California. He began following the games of the University of Southern California in 1926, and had not missed one by 1984, when he had seen 600 games, travelled 600,000 miles and spent $60,000.

Pro Bowl

Every year, representative teams from the NFC and AFC play each other in the Pro Bowl. The team rosters are chosen by votes, with team coaches, administrators and

▼ *The New York Giants show their muscle in team practice.*

journalists taking part, as well as the players. The game itself is more of a social occasion, although it gives fans the chance to see the best in action all at once.

Most Super Bowl victories

The most Super Bowl victories have been registered by Pittsburgh Steelers at four. Next come the Oakland/Los Angeles Raiders with three. The Miami Dolphins and Dallas Cowboys have made most appearances, at five.

Super Bowl awards

The team which wins the Super Bowl is awarded the Vince Lombardi Trophy (Lombardi was a famous Green Bay Packer coach). Made of sterling silver it is 20 inches high and weighs about 7 lb. A new one is made each year. Each player of the winning club receives a ring, of different design each year. They will usually contain diamonds and be worth several thousand dollars. But, as they are the top award in football, it is unlikely anybody would want to sell one.

Glossary

Blocking Legally obstructing an opposing player. A blocker is not allowed to hold on to another player with his hands, or to encircle or trip a player with his arms, and all blocks must be from the front. Not the same as tackling.

Chain crew The officials who operate the 10-yard measuring chain to settle yardage disputes.

Clipping Illegal blocking from the rear and below the waist.

Completion The legal acceptance of a forward pass.

Cut or cutback A change of direction by a runner.

Dead ball A ball that can no longer be advanced. Fouls committed after the ball has been whistled dead are called 'dead ball fouls'.

Defence The team without the ball, or that team's tactics.

Defensive backs Cornerbacks or safeties positioned in the defensive backfield area.

Delay of game The failure by the quarterback to start the game within the allowed 30 seconds.

Down A move or play from a line of scrimmage. The offensive team has four downs to gain 10 yards upfield. If the players succeed, they get the chance to play four more downs. If they fail, the ball passes to the other team, who become the offence for their own four downs.

End line The final line at each end of the field, at the back of the end zone.

End zone The area between the goal line, and the end line.

Extra point The point awarded when the ball is kicked through the goalposts after a touchdown – called a touchdown conversion. It is also known as the point after touchdown (PAT).

Fair catch Unhindered catch by receiver of a punt or kick off. Player raises his arm to signal his intention and cannot be touched or run with the ball.

Field goal A goal kicked from anywhere on the field, worth three points.

First down The 10 yards gained by the offense in their set of four downs. After this, the team gets another four downs.

Flag down An indication by an official, who throws down a yellow cloth, that a foul has been committed.

Free kick Any kick, including a kick-off, that puts the ball into play, for example, after a safety.

Goal line The line between the field of play and the end zone.

Handoff The handing of the ball by one player to another, usually the quarterback to running back.

Hash marks The lines running down the centre of the playing field which are used for spotting the ball.

Holding Illegally grasping an opponent with the hands.

Huddle When each of the teams form a group during the game so their quarterbacks can explain the play.

Ineligible receiver An offensive player who is not allowed to catch a forward pass.

Interception The catching of a pass by the defence.

Line of scrimmage The imaginary line from one sideline to the other, which crosses the place where a ball is spotted before a down. At the start of a down, the teams line up on either side of the line of scrimmage.

Measuring chain The chain which measures the yardage gained by the offensive team during a down.

Neutral zone An area, the length of the ball, between the offensive and defensive lines at the line of scrimmage.

Offence The team with the ball, or that team's tactics.

Offside The offence of crossing the line of scrimmage at the time the ball is snapped.

Pass pattern The route a receiver takes to get into position for a pass.

Personal foul An act of violence on an opposing player, carrying a heavy penalty.

Pitchout A pass, usually underhand, from a quarterback to a running back, as an alternative to the more usual handoff.

Punt A kick by the offence to gain space when they are unlikely to achieve another first down.

Punt return The distance gained by a player catching a punt and running back.

Safety (1) A play resulting in two points for the defence, most commonly: the ball carrier being tackled in his own end zone, the offence making a foul play in the end zone, or a missed direct snap to a punter crossing the end line. (2) A defensive back.

Scrimmage See Line of scrimmage.

Secondary The defensive backfield area, or the defensive backs within it.

Set (1) The offensive or defensive line formation. (2) The three-point stance of a lineman, leaning over, with one hand down on the ground.

Signals The coded messages called out by the quarterback to his team, to indicate the play at the line of scrimmage.

Snap The passing of the ball by the centre, nearly always to the quarterback, to initiate play at the line of scrimmage.

Special teams The teams brought in by both sides for the kicking plays: kick-off, punt, extra point and field goal attempts.

Spike The emphatic throwing of the ball to the ground to celebrate a touchdown.

Spot The placing of the ball by the referee, after a play or penalty, in preparation for the next down.

Sweep A wide run around the offensive line.

Tackle Bringing down or holding on to the ball carrier, thus bringing the play to an end. See also Blocking.

Time-out A temporary stop to the game, and the game clock, which can be called by either team or the referee. Each team is allowed to call three 90-second time-outs in each half. **Time-in** is when the clock is running.

Touchdown The principal scoring play – the act of crossing the goal line with the ball in a running play, or catching the ball in the end zone. It is worth six points.

Two-minute offence An offence launched usually in the last two minutes of the game, by a side needing to score and using time-saving ploys.

Two-minute warning The automatic time-out which allows officials to notify both sides that only two minutes remain in each half of the game.

Index

Acknowledgements

Illustrated by
Hayward Art Group
Hayward and Martin
Michael Roffe
RT Partners

Photographs supplied by
All Action/Duncan Raban p. 67
Bettman Archive Inc/BBC
Hulton Picture Library p. 15, 77
Colorsport p. 2, 5, 13, 18,
59, 61, 63, 65, 71
David Jefferis p. 63

Picture research by
Penny Warn

Text editing by
Angela Royston

Designed and edited by
Sunrise Books